Speed Reading: How t

Faster and Become an

Positive Psychology Coaching Series

Copyright © 2015 by Ian Tuhovsky

Author's blog: <u>www.mindfulnessforsuccess.com</u>

Table of Contents:

My Free Gift to You

Discover How to Get Rid of Stress & Anxiety and Reach Inner Peace in 20 Days or Less!

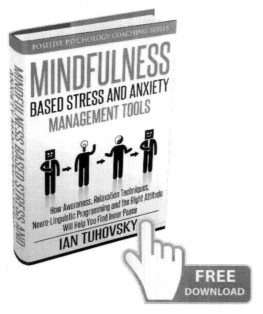

To help speed up your personal transformation, I have prepared a special gift for you!

Download my full, 120 page e-book "Mindfulness Based Stress and Anxiety Management Tools" (Value: $9.99) for free.

Moreover, by becoming my subscriber, you will be the first one to **get my new books for only $0.99,** during their short two day promotional launch. **I passionately write about**: social dynamics, career, Neuro-Linguistic Programming, goal achieving, positive psychology and philosophy, life hacking, meditation and becoming the most awesome version of yourself. Additionally, once a week I will send you insightful tips and **free e-book offers** to keep you on track on your journey to becoming the best you!

That's my way of saying **"thank you"** to my new and established readers and helping you grow. I hate spam and e-mails that come too frequently – **you will never receive more than one email a week! Guaranteed.**

Just follow this link:
http://www.mindfulnessforsuccess.com/positive-psychology-coaching/giveaway.html

Please be aware that every e-book and "short read" I publish is written truly by me, with thoroughly researched content 100% of the time. Unfortunately, there's a huge number of low quality, cheaply outsourced spam titles on Kindle non-fiction market these days, created by various Internet marketing companies. I don't tolerate these books. I want to provide you with high quality, so <u>if you think that one of my books/short reads can be improved anyhow, please contact me at:</u>

contact@mindfulnessforsuccess.com

<u>I will be very happy to hear from you, because that's who I write my books for!</u>

Introduction

"...there have been gazillions of people that have lived before all of us. There's no new problem you could have - with your parents, with school, with a bully. There's no new problem that someone hasn't already had and written about it in a book." – Will Smith

Reading is one of the most important skills for those who want to really succeed in life. No matter if your objective is to do great during your University exams, become a bestselling writer, or start your own business, you will have to read A LOT, and I mean it. Reading takes time. Time is our most valuable asset - nothing new here. You can always make money or meet new friends, but you will never be able to "make time". The only way to succeed and have a happy life without regrets is to use it wisely and learn how to manage and save it.

How fast do you really read? Do you have an idea of the ways by which you can increase your speed of reading tremendously?

In this book, I will take you through the dynamics of speed reading in a way you may have never imagined before. I'm here to preach the need for speed reading and make use of some of the principles that can steer your knowledge and productivity in the right direction.

I'm going to share with you the methods that I used. There are many, so everyone will find their way. This book has been designed to offer you the best points of a tried and tested formula – straight to the point, with no fluff and fillers. Regardless of the speed at which you read the text, this book is going to bring in transformation and change which will make your life easier. We are going to hack your brain a little and update your habits. Reinstall your reading system. When you can read lengthy texts in no time and comprehend the matter as well, the type of impression it will put on others and the change it will make in your life is going to be truly exceptional. So, what are you waiting for? Check out the ways, perfect the techniques and become a speed reader in a very small time frame.

Chapter 1: An Insight Into Speed Reading

"It is what you read when you don't have to do that determines what you will be when you can't help it." – Oscar Wilde

I remember the times when I used to curl on my bed and cry myself to sleep. I used to be a very slow reader in my early years. Elementary school could be a tormenting place for someone who could not catch up fast. I had a few friends who stood by my side, but it was a tough battle anyways.

It was my dad who told me about speed reading techniques, and it was one thing I desperately wanted to master. My dad came up with the idea of reading me books, at least an hour a day, before sleep. This way I learned to read very fast and after one year I overtook my peers, becoming the fastest reader in my class. Things stayed that way until high school.

Tell me, when was the last time you were learning how to read? It was the last time you learned how to read at all, correct? Kindergarten or elementary school - Dr. Seuss, Chronicles of Narnia, Hatchet or Robinson Crusoe – all nice, fun and easy to read. Then comes high school and University – biology, engineering, chemistry – difficult terms, lots of material you don't want to read, but can't avoid it – a big game changer. Moreover - after age of twelve, most people stop improving their reading speed. You would say that it should continually increase as you're developing, but in most cases that's not true. It's like you wanted to become a pro downhill biker with your silly 4-wheeled children's bicycle. You need to change your gear.

Lots of reading during high school and the strategies I used to apply turned out insufficient. I had to come up with new ways and ideas. More than that, I knew lots of people who stayed awake late at night too many times because they took a long time to ace the lessons. As their reading speed was terribly slow, it was hard for them to cover the material and they ended up doing "night sessions". Further, owing to the lack of proper sleep, they were exhausted and could not focus during the exams. Ultimately, they failed too many times and had to repeat classes. This has an overall cumulative effect and has the power to wreck the confidence of people as well. The amount of books you need to read to cover your syllabus can be whopping, especially if you're studying engineering, medicine, psychology, law etc.

When you are looking to graduate with good credits, it is important that you can cover as much knowledge as possible and REMEMBER it. If you are a slow reader, you will find it hard to take out that much time from your schedule. However, as a speed reader, you will be able to cover a lot of lessons in little time, and thus you can read even more and supplement your knowledge base.

Speed reading can help you get rid of all the above mentioned problems. I started doing my bit because I knew I had to master this art if I wanted to graduate at all. I won't exaggerate and tell you that it was an overnight change, because it was not. There were days when I thought I was making no progress, but then days over days, the layers of change kept piling. Today, I have an awesome count of words per minute and my life become much easier.

Not only were my classmates in awe of the changes I managed to make (I organized a short speed-reading course at my university, which was my first win-win type business), but at the same time, I can now save a lot of time too. I can read material in nearly half the time (or sometimes much faster) and devote the rest of the time either to my family or to my hobbies. One of the best aspects of speed reading is that not only do I read fast, but I can comprehend a lot quickly too. I love the positive changes speed reading has brought in my life.

The History of Speed Reading

The United States Air Force was the first one to get an insight into the speed reading techniques. They use the tachistoscope which is a device that was used to display an image only for a specified amount of time. Though the concept originated from this, it was not until the 1950s that speed reading was fully conceptualized.

It was Evelyn Wood who took up the task of understanding why some people could read faster than others. After she got a clear understanding of the same, she started teaching her techniques in university of Utah and thus spearheaded the speed reading movements.

If you look at the presidents of America, you will find that John F. Kennedy developed a reading speed of 1200 words per minute. Can you even imagine the kind of speed that is? Comprehend the amount of little time he would take to complete a big book? It is without a doubt an extraordinary speed. Kennedy wasn't the only president with such exceptional reading record.

Apart from this, President Jimmy Carter opted to have speed reading classes inside the White House. He used to take these classes along with his family. There are also reports that president George Washington was a natural speed reader.

Hence, speed reading as a habit, has always interested a lot of people and managed to excite too many of us, including the eminent personalities as well.

Debunking Popular Myths

Let's now deal with the most popular myths about speed reading. I will expand more on some of these topics later in this book.

-**Reading faster reduces your ability to memorize: NOT TRUE.** Guess who will be the first one to tell you this kind of B.S? Yep - people who read ridiculously slowly and think that reading is a tiresome and tedious activity. Do you really think that guys who torture themselves over each single word or sentence, subsequently getting more tired and angry do have better results? Sorry, that's not the way it is. Speed reading techniques and habits will boost your comprehension and ability to memorize, period. The faster you can understand something, the deeper your focus gets.

-**All parts of book are equally important – NOT TRUE.** I came to this realization when I published my first book in Europe. I had to put some fluff in that one – unnecessary pictures, diagrams, charts, comic strips (!) and a few short chapters, just because my publisher thought that would be brilliant. It's like all these lofty headmaster's speeches we had to go through during school, wishing that we could fast forward them to the main point. While reading, you actually can push the *FF* button.

-**Reading is continuous – NOT TRUE.** I used to think that reading always requires you to start at the beginning of each part and then treadmill through the chapter, necessarily in the order the book was pieced together. Actually, there are many other better ways of going through your material.

-Reading is "word to word" process – NOT TRUE. It was a good idea in elementary school. Now you need different techniques. You can easily read whole sentences or paragraphs in no time if you put some effort in your training – in a sentence, we are looking for the meaning, not single words.

-The average reading speed is the best for learning as it's natural – NOT TRUE. Your average reading speed is **not natural.** It's just a result of methods that you have been using so far and their limitations.

The Things To Expect

Did you get excited about speed reading? Do you want to excel in this art too? There are a few things you need to expect and the ones you may not. Here is a snapshot of the same.

- Speed reading is not a "magic pill". You should not expect to get the changes overnight.

- Some people are going to be naturally fast readers. This does not means that slow readers can never pace up.

- Speed reading techniques are diverse and involve change of habits which is a major part; however, they do involve mind games/techniques as well.

- Speed reading doesn't merely focus on how fast you can read words/sentences. You have to concentrate upon comprehending and remembering the text you read too.

- Your eye span plays one of the most important roles.

- A change of habit mostly takes time and you have to keep working hard and consistently until your goal has been finally achieved.

Chapter 2: Environment and Preparation

Let's now start. Remember, this is not a book merely meant for reading. Here, you need to assimilate the points, follow the details and keep practicing. Just like you won't learn how to dance or juggle just by reading a book about it, so you won't become a speed reader if you won't stick to your training of Speed, Comprehension and Recall. Now, let's begin starting with the basics.

The reading environment and preparation

There are people who are gifted enough to read in all kinds of environment, but when you are learning speed reading techniques, it is best advised to choose a befitting reading environment. Speed reading demands a lot of concentration. Unfortunately, our concentration (as a whole mankind) decreased significantly during last thirty years, as well as our reading speed. Some computer games and materials available on-line should add to our speed and comprehension, but unfortunately, obtrusive TV watching, ever present radio, social media as well as checking our phones and e-mails every five seconds doesn't really help. Our minds go haywire and we don't even know it.

Even the slightest slip in your attention span can be deterrent and this is the key reason as to why you need to know how to choose an apt environment. OK, let's now focus on the most important aspects of your preparation.

Before you start your reading session, make sure that:

1. No one will disrupt you – tell your friends/family that e.g. you're going to learn for important exams or that you just really need to focus and they should leave you alone. Silence your phone if you're not waiting for any really important news. Also, try to avoid open spaces and moving objects – sitting on your balcony or terrace may distract you. We are all naturally wired to pay attention to the objects that are changing position. Ideally, when you are at your desk reading, the wall in front of you should have a single solid color as this will improve your attention span.

2. You turned off music, TV, radio. You can try listening to a quiet classical or electronic ambient music as well as to binaural waves (search for "learning binaural waves" / "learning aid" in YouTube) or a brown/pink noise (**http://tinyurl.com/binauralsaid**) which is good for

concentration and eliminates noises around you. You can also try records of nature sounds, **BUT I really recommend that you <u>try reading in absolute silence</u>, especially if you're a beginner to this.**

3. You turned off your computer to avoid distractions – especially Internet, social media etc. The only thing that you need is your material/book, a pen or a marker, another book or a piece of paper (for "Hide and Read" technique) and **a bottle of plain mineral water.** I will tell you about the importance of being properly hydrated later in this book. You should also use a timer. The good idea would be to also have a smart phone with a digital dictionary on your desk, which is much faster and more convenient to use than a traditional dictionary book. Each time you're stuck with a word or phrase you don't know, it's going to slow you down and distract your focus – this is when this kind of software really helps.

4. You don't sit in a stuffy or cold/hot room. Make sure that you have fresh air to breathe. If it's too hot, use a fan. If it's too cold, use a heater. Proper breathing and hydration are crucial to your focus and speed reading. It may seem obvious, but you would be extremely surprised how many people ignore this simple rule...You can easily forget about letting the fresh air to your room when you're focused on reading, just to find out later that you hardly remembered anything. The devil is in the details!

5. You took time to get rid of all unsolved business before you start reading/learning. If you have problems, try to get rid of them first, or just make a first step, so that you can feel easy during your

reading session. It sounds simple, yet it's a very important point. I remember how hard it was to learn for exam every time I had argued with someone or didn't want to take care of my health first (e.g. visit a dentist) etc. Make your business straight out first if you can. If you can't, then don't obsess about it. You're just wasting your time. The only moment for a change is NOW. A peace of mind is crucial.

6. The place is bright enough. Don't strain your vision, you just have one! Also, if the light is not adjusted correctly, your brain will have to put additional effort in reading without you even knowing about it. You will just feel tired and sleepy. Headaches are also very likely. Even if you manage to read your material, you won't be really likely to remember most of it. The same goes to defect of visions. So:

   - Have your glasses (cleaned well)/contact lenses on (make sure that they are "up to date" with your eyes, visit your doctor!) or decide for a laser operation which will reduce your defect - if you can afford it and if it's possible. It will make reading much easier.

   - Make sure that your room is bright enough (I use 100 watt bulb in a personal lamp with a bendable neck + additional lamp on the ceiling, but better ask your doctor what's the best solution for you) and the light falls right on your book from the correct angle (so that it's not too bright, you sight should remain relaxed, not irritated) or that screen of the device you're reading on is bright enough. Also, try not to mix sunlight with electric light. It's not too good for your eyes and your concentration.

7. Your posture is correct. Don't lie down with your book, don't read on your bed, and don't read on your carpet. It will make you sleepy and lazy. Choose one spot and make it your workplace. After time, your brain will "link" that place to learning and you will be more alert anytime you sit there. It's called *anchoring*. Moreover:

   - Don't sit on a chair, looking on the book lying flat on your desk. It will make you sleepy as well. Your book/device should be angled.

   - Ideally, you should sit on a wooden or office chair. There's no such thing as "ideal posture for everyone", but you can read these short articles online, they may give you some good ideas:

   http://tinyurl.com/readingposture

   http://tinyurl.com/readingposture2

8. You try not to stay up overnight. Sleep is very important and I will be writing about this topic later. For now – remember that sunlight makes you naturally awake (even when the sky is cloudy). Try to learn when it's naturally bright outside and sleep when it's dark if possible. Note that it may be quite difficult if you live above the Arctic Circle, but you get the point. Starting your session while you're sleepy won't help neither.

9. Try not to read just right after something important (of a big emotional charge) happened. It will be difficult to focus if you have just proposed to your girlfriend or won few thousand dollars in a lottery. Not that I don't wish you great relationships or luck, on the contrary :-)! But keep that rule in mind - I can remember that reading right after I found out how great the last exam had went was really difficult. I had to go for a walk and calm down or celebrate and start the next day. On the other hand – ask yourself if you're not just looking for excuses.

10. You know why are you reading – before you start, ask yourself these three questions:

    1. Why do you need to read this?

    2. Exactly what information do you have to obtain?

    3. What do you currently know about the topic?

Now, this step is **VERY** important. The first question gives you motivation and momentum, kicks your butt, and sets your priorities right. We, humans, naturally avoid unnecessary work. In fact, every being in the universe tends to save energy as much as possible. You have to give your mind A REASON to do the work. That's why a good idea would be to write the reason down on a piece of paper or say it aloud.

The second question enables you to focus EXACTLY on what you need to focus on right now. The third question allows you to skip the parts of the material you may be already familiar with, makes both your selection and skimming more accurate.

So many times I spent countless hours on reading material or a book without asking myself these three crucial questions just to find out later how much time had I lost without really learning anything at all, or reading things that I already knew.

11. Last one thing- breathing. Most people are shallow breathers. We don't breathe deep enough. Our brains don't work at their full potential and aren't even close to it. You need enough fresh oxygen if you want to be a speed reader and learn effectively. Before you even start, you should relax and concentrate. You may want to make use of this technique. You just need 8-10 minutes to bring your energy levels up:

- Set your alarm clock for eight minutes.

- Sit down on a chair with your back straight and your hands on your lap, with your feet on the ground/carpet. Keep your chin slightly raised.

- Close your eyes.

- Focus on breathing. Begin breathing slowly and deeply, inhaling and exhaling through your nose. Take eight deep breaths, hold each for about four seconds. You can count in your mind. *One... two... three... four...*

- After that, let your breath adjust naturally- it should still be deep, but not too deep. It should feel comfortable and relaxing.

- Breathe. As you exhale, say "release" in your mind and feel the tension leaving your body. Hold each breath for about two seconds.

- After eight breaths, start imagining how the air your inhale is green or sky-blue and how it fills your lungs and then your whole body with a gentle, warm energy. As you exhale, imagine red air leaving your body, taking away all the bad emotions, distractions and mental/physical discomfort. Hold each breath for a few seconds.

- You can also imagine the colorful air filling your brain and helping you concentrate. You can also repeat in your mind: "I'm a good learner, I can read fast and remember everything". I know that it may sound silly, odd or even dumb to you but really - it works every time I do it and it works for my friends and family too.

- You should ideally do this exercise for eight minutes, but you can also extend it to ten minutes.

- After you finish, you can stand up, jump few times, rock your shoulders, twist your head few times all around your neck, wash your face with cool water and then get to reading.

When you have a favorable environment and preparation ritual that will help you in concentrating on your material, it is likely to improve your reading speed. With the right kind of environment that is free of noise and distractions, it will be easier for you to concentrate on the speed reading techniques which we will be discussing subsequently. Now, let's get to the serious business!

Chapter 3: Key Speed Reading Techniques

Before we even start with exercises, you should be aware of your actual reading speed and know how to measure it. The average person reads from one hundred fifty to two hundred words a minute (WPM) – the estimation is based on the so called "average material", which means that when you're reading something easy, e.g. a fairy tale or a thriller that you already know, you speed will be slightly higher. On the other hand – when reading a material full of technical terms, you will have to slow down a little – let's say to one hundred words per minute. But here's a twist – the measurements are based on the one minute reading sessions. I highly doubt that you take a break every sixty seconds – that would be highly ineffective and not too natural. So after extended time of reading, your productivity and focus usually take a nose-dive. So, looking at this matter realistically – the average reading speed is even lower than these one hundred fifty or two hundred words per minute. Like I said in the previous chapter, our speed decreased – thirty years ago it was about three hundred fifty words per minute.

So how do you measure your reading speed? You can do it yourself, but come on, we live in the 21st century. Just follow these links, and you can check your reading speed right now:

http://tinyurl.com/measureyourspeed - here you can measure both your speed and comprehension.

http://www.myreadspeed.com/calculate/ - here you can choose excerpt that you want to read. It will record your reading speed nicely as well.

In case you're offline at the moment and you just can't wait to figure it out, here it is:

-Take an article or a book, something rather "neutral" to you would be the best (don't pick an economy book if you hate economy) – let's say an article in the magazine that you like to read occasionally.

-Read for one minute. Set your timer. Don't try to go too fast here, you're not going to impress me, I can't even see you :- (and it won't help you either. Read naturally, just like you always do.

-Mark whenever you stopped in the text.

-Then you have to figure out how many words are there per line on average: take three full lines and count all the words, then divide the number by three.

-Multiply the average number of words per line by the number of lines you read. This will give you the number of words per minute that you just read. It won't be 100% precise – to make it so, you would need to count every single word in the text that you just read – but it can give you good general idea.

Mind you that your reading speed is not a constant – it is lower when you're sleepy, higher when you're calm and happy etc. But nevertheless – take these tests and write down your reading speed somewhere in a notebook. You should get one now and write down your progress, day after day. It will keep you going.

OK - let's now proceed to the techniques and ideas that helped me.

Attention Holds The Key

Whenever you are doing something that involves speed, attention and concentration become doubly important. If you let your attention slip away, it is never going to bring in the results for you. Think of a situation where you are reading an article on the economic times but your attention is focused on the super bowl match you saw last night. Are you ever going to assimilate the content of the article?

Whenever your attention slips, your speed of reading and your ability to comprehend the text is going to suffer miserably.

One common flaw among readers is to look at the lines below your current text. This is a perfect recipe for slowing your speed and losing your attention as well. If you want to get rid of these troubles, use this simple and yet extremely effective technique.

Hide and Read

You can keep your hands or even a piece of paper and any other object to hide the lines that are below the ones you are reading. The main problem is that owing to the increased inquisitiveness of knowing what awaits you, you fail to get an idea of what you are currently reading. This will require a second read of the current paragraph and thus your overall speed cuts down significantly. When I stumbled upon this method I immediately knew it was going to solve my problem.

Having this obstruction will prevent you from reading lines which you don't need to. When you are fully focused just on reading the line you are meant to, it really helps. An important tip which you have to bear in mind is that you should be smooth in moving the obstruction object. If you take a lot of time sliding it down when you are reading, it will end up killing your time. So be smooth in your movements and push down the object as and when you read the lines.

When you are unable to hide the lines in an apt manner, you can use other techniques as well. There are people who use their hands for the sake of covering the texts. You should keep on sliding your hands as you are reading. When you are reading texts on the computer, you can use features like auto scroll as it is one way of focusing on current text rather than beholding the one which is located below your current passage.

Use a Pacer

This is one of the foundational ideas for the sake of improving your speed and will especially be of use for those who have a habit of getting distracted. It is different than Hide and Read as not only is it keeping the lines below from your sight, but it's also making you read faster. You can significantly improve your reading speed right now just using a sharp pointed object like a marker or even a pencil or your finger and use it pinpoint to the specific area where you are reading (I use my fountain pen). This will either partially or completely obstruct your view of the subsequent paragraphs. With a pacer it is nearly impossible to lose your place on a page. Moreover, whenever you point to something, you're ordering your brain to pay attention to it. The same goes to moving objects. We are naturally wired this way, so why not make use of our natural instincts?

If your attention still wavers in varying direction, you can use a bigger (bright and colourful) marker, or your hands, to cover the below portion and keep moving them as and when you read. It's like using a pacer and *Hide and Read* technique at the same time.

This won't be possible when you are reading online because you cannot really cover the screen with your hands. In such cases, you should fall back upon your mouse pointer and try to concentrate a little harder when you are reading.

But have no fear, my fellow reader! Here I have come up with some nice patents that you can use when reading on your computer or tablet.

Reading Tips for Computer and Tablet

1. Reformatting – I can remember that whenever I found texts online that were difficult to read, I would skip them. That wasn't a good idea, because I had to waste more time on further research. What you can do instead is to simply copy the text and paste it to your text processor and reformat it so that it's easier to read – pick different fonts, change colors, make it bigger, adjust spacing etc. You can also print it and use your finger, pen or a card (Hide and Read). On the other hand, you should think for a moment before you do that, because that will consume some of your time too, and if the info is easily accessible on many other websites, that would make no sense. Use it whenever you find a rare piece of info on a website that is distracting – I have once found great economic data I'd almost die for on a website that somehow survived in an unchanged "design" since 1995. Imagine all the cheesy flashy gifs and yellow comic sans font contrasting with black-ish animated wallpaper on the background.

2. Automatic mouse scrolling – you can also use scrolling to make your reading session easier. Simply use scroll button (it's usually the wheel in the middle of your mouse, you should

be able to press it) to steer through your document at the speed that is appropriate for you. If it's automatic (and it usually is), you can just sit back and read when the text is scrolling itself on your screen. If you're not sure how to do it, ask someone who's more into computers to show you. Just tell them what you want to achieve and then test different speeds. It's very useful.

3. Highlighting – just like you can use a pen or finger as a pacer when reading on paper, you can use highlighting on a website or in your text editor to significantly accelerate your reading speed. Just click right where you want to start reading, and drag your mouse pointer to highlight sentences as you read. After each paragraph, click to clear the previous highlight and start again. Simple and very effective. Just be sure that you won't press delete button while most of your document is selected in your text editor. Use this technique when your file is saved, when you can use the "redo" option or it is on "read only" mode.

4. Use your screen edge for *Hide and Read* technique: Just scroll the text so that the first sentence that you want to read is the last sentence visible on your screen, and then scroll as you want to read next sentence, e.g. scrolling manually or automatically. This way you won't be distracted by the next paragraphs and sentences. Extremely easy, yet few people do it.

5. Use software or special websites – which I will present to you later in this book.

Don't Speak the Words Aloud – Quit Vocalization

It is extremely common for most people to speak out the words loud when reading them. A lot of people are of the opinion that doing so helps them in improving their understanding of the passage, because they were taught so in elementary school. However, when you are looking to grasp the ideas of speed reading, you need to know that this is one of the key mistakes that end up slowing you down.

If you want to speed up, you have to learn how to read without mouthing the words – both verbally and in your head. While your reading speed can rise tremendously high, there is a limit up to which you can speak the words out loud or in your thoughts. This is a limitation you need to work upon.

This is not going to be an extremely easy task to do for the simple reason that if you already have a habit of doing so, it can be a hard one to unlearn. However, you need to keep trying and changes will come up over a period of time. The awareness of your vocalization alone will help you a lot.

Very often your reading comprehensibility may be impacted because of the change. However, when you keep trying and start reading without the need to vocalize the words; you will soon be able to have the right comprehensibility (I'd say that it will be much, much better than before) even without the need to speak the words. When doing so, your eyes simply need to just skim through the content and your reading speed is much more likely to increase. Now you're limited just to speed of your eyes and your comprehension skills, and they can be trained significantly. You are not slowing yourself down.

Let me know show you this very simple and great exercise – take a medium-difficulty text, start reading it at your average, natural speed. Then, as you read, start going "lalalala" in your head or aloud. Do this for at least four minutes per reading session. You will immediately realize that you can understand the text anyways and so often it will enable you to read faster, as you won't be slowing down to vocalize. Your comprehension might fall a little while doing so, but it will come with practice.

Skimming

Skimming refers to jumping over some words and lines and reading the content in a way that you catch the important parts and skip the ones that are not desired.

Speed reading should be about understanding the vast majority of what you read (100% of the crucial content), but sometimes you just have to make a quick preview of what's in front of you, without going into too much detail. This technique is great when you don't have enough time, or you just have to learn something to obtain necessary information, but you don't enjoy it. When you are going through a piece of text, you are sure to know that not every word of it has to be read to comprehend the meaning in its entirety. When you're skimming, you are going to read three to four times faster, so obviously your understanding will decrease significantly, especially at the beginning of your speed-reading adventure. When you're reading on the computer/tablet screen you will have to slow down a bit as it's more difficult.

Now, let's do an experiment. Take any lengthy or a medium article. If paragraph separation is well visible, that's a perfect one.

Now – please look at the first sentence in the first paragraph. Does it look like a main topic idea of the whole paragraph? I guess so. It's probably like: "here's what I'm going to tell you about in the next sentences."

Then take a look at the first sentence from next paragraph. Most of times (about 70%), the first sentence will tell you what the whole paragraph is going to be about.

Of course, it's not always THAT simple. Some authors are big babblers and they need to tell you this and that before they get to the point, or before they even start introducing the main idea. Just like you don't go fast with your car all the time, sometimes you have to slow down when speed reading. Knowing that, when you go through the text fast using your pen or hand, you should **slow down on every first sentence of each paragraph.** Then go back to skimming faster until next paragraph. Always look for the main purpose of each paragraph. When you know it, you know the topic and so you can find the main sentence much faster. Using this simple technique you can skim through articles and chapters rapidly, without losing your comprehension.

Another important thing is that you should remember why you are skimming. Remember the question from point number ten of the last chapter? "Why do you need to read this"? If you want to be effective here, you need to remember what info exactly you are looking for. If you don't, you will just get sleepy, lose your focus and your time reading all the things that you don't need to.

Make a Preview

This is another idea that can be extremely useful. You should ideally make a preview of the lesson you are about to read - quickly browsing each page to make a quick map in your mind of what are you just about to read. At this point you will be able to initially see which parts you will be able to skip totally or skim faster, and which will require your strong focus.

While this may entail a slightly larger time because you are going through the content without actually reading it; this will give you an improved kick start into reading the text and actually REMEMBERING it and prepare you for what the article will speak about. When you are making a preview of the article you meant to read, you should not waste too much time in doing so. Once you have done a preview, you are likely to improve the speed with which you can skim over the contents. Moreover, repetition makes you remember things better – do you know lyrics of your favorite songs or the whole lengthy scenes from your favorite movies or TV series? That's it.

The idea about the preview is merely to gauge the flow of the topic and have some prior idea regarding what the entire text is going to be. If you are unsure as to how you need to approach this technique, here are some tips that can be helpful for you.

1. When you are merely gazing at the article, try and gauge the genre in which it falls. This is a crucial step and make sure you don't go wrong here. Merely reading the first line, a few snippets from the paragraphs in between and the conclusion should give you the clear idea of the genre of article. Pay attention to the introductory paragraphs and read them carefully – they could be either "stuffed" at the very beginning of the article or in each chapter's introduction. They will help you in building both your "map" and your comprehension of the whole material.

2. If it is a genre that fits your field of interest, you do not really need a very detailed preview. When you are reading things that you like, your speed of reading will be high. However, if you find that the genre isn't really something that will perk your interest, be more thorough with the preview.

3. When you are making a preview, you should ideally divide the articles into different segments. Pick a line each from every paragraph as it will give you an idea of what to expect from each paragraph.

4. You do not have to read all the sentences when you are making a preview. If you are attentive, reading them once should help you grasp the content. Previewing is merely taking a glance and

skimming very roughly. It gives you a mind snapshot of what the content is without actually reading the exact structure and details of the same. Upon repeated execution, it is sure to turn out to be an extremely useful tool.

5. Spend no more than ten minutes on previewing, unless the material of a REALLY large volume, but try to keep it short anyways.

Follow these steps in a systematic manner and it will help you get better at previewing the articles and making the most out of it. With a clear and through preview, you can improve your reading speed substantially.

Also notice that often times you can save time by skipping examples. Usually they're used to convince readers to something. If you believe in author's expertise or their point, you can just skip them.

Moreover, you don't have to finish sentences when skimming – so often you can be sure that a sentence won't give you the info you are looking for just by reading first few words or see if it's just a filler or author's divagation. If it's a book that we are talking about, or a lengthy article - you should be able to get into author's shoes after a few chapters/sections and start seeing his patterns of writing – so that you will be able to sense which parts should be skipped and which investigated into.

One of the problems a lot of people face when they are skimming contents is that they fail to tell the parts to skim from the ones which are important. To avoid this problem, the best solution is to initially choose reading topics that pertain to your interest. It will be easier for you to exercise.

It is a psychological fact that when you are reading something which you are interested in, your concentration and attention is going to be very high. This will help you get a view of the things that are important. Once you master the skimming exercise by using your favorite content, you can then move to genres that do not fall in your interest area.

Skimming and Diagrams

Here's another important strategy. When reading articles and books, so often you are going to run into diagrams or charts etc. that you have to analyze and understand. They often contain crucial data. Unfortunately, some diagrams can be extremely convoluted. Now, most people have very bad approach here. When they read a paragraph that directs them to a certain diagram (e.g. *go to fig. 3.8*) they either go like "ah, okay, I will do it later, let me finish this paragraph first", or they take a quick glance at it, can't understand it, go back to the paragraph, read it again, then go back to the diagram, can't understand it again, go back to the text…etc. A vicious circle and a massive waste of time and energy.

What you should do instead is, whenever you run into information that is directing you to a chart/diagram or a picture, STOP READING immediately and go to the diagram. Take a first glance, try to figure it out and then go back to text (you can leave your finger at the place you just stopped reading, so you don't get lost). If it's referring to the diagram now, read the sentence and then go back to the diagram, looking for the confirmation of what you just read. Then read another sentence, look at the diagram again, look for the info you that just read about.

An image is so often worth more than thousands of words. That may look like an inconvenient way of reading, and you may have the impression that it's slowing you down, but it's a very effective strategy. It doesn't leave you confused and it's ultimately much faster. Moreover, whenever you can see the information that you just read visually, it increases your comprehension insanely. So, anytime there's a reference to a picture or a chart in your text, you want to "slice" your reading a bit and start jumping between the chart and the paragraph that you're reading, until they stop referring to it. When it comes to footnotes – you should read them if you need to learn the material thoroughly. If you don't, you can just go to every footnote as you read the text and quickly scan it/skim it to check if there's any usable info.

Skimming and Taking Notes

Taking notes is one of the best learning and comprehension techniques, especially when skimming, however you should keep in mind that it needs to be balanced properly.

Some people take too many notes, while others don't take enough. Your notes should be organized in numbered bullet points and be like a quick summary of each paragraph. One-two sentences, usually no more.

The mistake I used to make was practically re-writing the whole material. While it can be helpful when you don't have too much to learn, it's a big obstacle when you have big piles to read. The same goes to highlighting- it is **very** helpful – but not when you're highlighting the whole page! Yes, I was guilty of that too.

So my advice is - when taking a note or highlighting, **finish reading a paragraph first.** Note down or highlight only the CRUCIAL sentences. Sometimes you should only mark one word that will bring you back to the main idea. You should REMEMBER the material, and your notes should be like internet links or icon shortcuts sending you to each idea in your memory. For me, the most effective way of taking notes is to draw mind maps. If you're not sure how to take them, you should read this short article:

http://www.wikihow.com/Make-a-Mind-Map

You should also utilize this effective exercise:

1. Read a paragraph

2. Take a BRIEF note. The shorter and clearer - the better.

3. Read another paragraph, take a note, repeat.

To do that, you should always have pen at your hand when reading. If you do it frequently enough (even if you're not learning, but reading just for fun!) you will develop two very important habits: first of all, you will learn to ask yourself "what have I just read, what is it about?" and secondly, you will learn how to make a quick and short summary of long paragraphs. You should ideally do this twenty minutes a day for three weeks.

Moreover, you should always write down the most important key notes at the front of your book (if you can do it, of course). Someone said that you either use new information or lose it in thirty minutes. It will be much easier to remind yourself anytime you use this book.

Backtracking…

…is a habit that you have to eliminate completely! Every time you are reading a line, just to eventually skip back a few words or lines to re-read them, you are backtracking. It happens to almost everyone who is not familiar with the art of speed reading. So often we do it subconsciously. If you're not sure about it, you can ask someone to watch your eyes while you're reading a long text. But trust me when I say that 99% of "average readers" do it. The only way to stop this habit is to admit that you do it and… stop doing so. First of all, it ruins your fluency of thoughts and destroys your mental processes. Secondly, it consumes a lot of your time and eventually makes you feel tired. Third of all, you don't need to skip back at all. Really. When you watch a movie and you don't understand a scene just yet, do you rewind it to watch the scene again, or do you keep watching, as you are sure that it will become clear later?

Yeah, I didn't think so. **You just need to read faster, use a pacer and keep a constant rate of reading!**

Let me now show you another thing that will save you massive time. Have you ever read a sentence or a paragraph fifteen times in a row, just to eventually skip it anyways due to the lack of understanding? I bet you have. From now on, I recommend that when you bump into a difficult paragraph during your reading session (like "what was that I just read, I have no clue?" or "I don't understand it entirely"), just mark it (e.g. draw "X" on the margin) and then keep reading. When you finish reading a chapter, just go back, look at all the marks you've made, and reread these paragraphs. Nine times out of ten, it will be easier to understand, as you read the entire chapter and can refer it to the bigger picture and the complete context. So often certain sentences don't make sense at all until you finish reading the whole paragraph.

Skimming on Tests

When you're doing a reading test, so often you don't have time to read the whole thing.

Usually, both on SAT and ACT tests (and many others), you have a long passage of text, and then the questions. What people normally do is they read the whole test and then answer the questions. Some read the questions first, and then the passage.

What I recommend is that, as mentioned earlier, instead of reading the whole text at once, you start by reading the first sentence of every single paragraph- then take a look at your questions. Then, lastly, read the whole text. You will be able to understand it much better and remember more.

Technical Terms & Things Not So Easy to Remember

While reading, so often you will have to deal with technical terms or abstract words. First of all – you will have to make use of your dictionary (there are lots of technical dictionaries online to download to your smart phone or computer). Second of all- you will have to utilize some simple memory techniques to remember these words and terms.

Have you ever heard about the Baker-Baker paradox? During a study conducted to see how would someone remember names, people were introduced to someone named Mr. Baker. They didn't know it was a part of the experiment. The next day they were asked about the person's name – the vast majority of participants forgot it.

Now, there was another group, and they've been told that this guy's occupation was a baker. Almost everyone remembered. That's interesting as it's exactly the same word, just the context is different. Why does that happen?

The answer is quite simple – while thinking about "baker", you start visualizing the look – e.g. white uniform, hat, gloves etc. So – the more visual references, the more connections are being made in your brain. Knowing that, you can learn technical terms much easier. You can use the power of associations.

For example - acronyms, high school history lessons:
KGB sounds similar to "caged bee", so you can just imagine it and use to remember the acronym instantly. Or remember that an angry bee can be very dangerous, and the KGB was too.

RFN sounds a little bit like "ore fan". A big fan that cools down freshly melted metal ore in a shipyard. Can you imagine that? If not, you can try with a fan of *Oregon Ducks* with his face painted green. The possibilities are countless.

BJHS sound almost like "Bee Gee's a chess". You can imagine micro Bee Gees dancing on a chess board and singing: "Ah-ha-ha-ha, stayin' alive, stayin' alive!..." I agree that it sound extremely ridiculous, but **the more outstanding and funny your visualizations are, the better and easier they will be to remember.**

You can also similarly deal with other words, e.g. *Amathophobia* - a fear of dust. Sounds like a-moth-o-phobia. You can imagine that someone is afraid of moths, as their wings, just like butterfly wings, are all covered in dust. Or *Gamophobia* – fear of commitments – you can imagine that some guy is afraid of a marriage as it will be "game over" for his dating life and he won't be able to play computer games all nights.

You can also take a part of a word, think if it sounds similar to anything else and then come up with a short story or a rhyme (even the silliest) to remember complicated terms easier.

You should be ideally able to come up with these kinds of associations very fast, it will be a great use during your speed reading sessions. Exercise this kind of thinking and seeing things whenever you read anything. You should also practice this when you're reading fiction books, to remember names of characters or places.

Improve Your Eye Span + Use Peripheral Vision

This is by far one of the most effective and useful strategies that you can use for the sake of improving your reading speed. One of the major limitations when you are reading is your eye span. Obviously, we can only read as many words as we can see. You have to practice movements which will help you improve your eye span. The focus is to improve the number of words that you see in a single glance. When we are reading a text, we have to continuously keep moving our eye span and the larger it is, the faster we will read.

All those who can read fast have a larger eye span. You can increase it by continuous practice as well. Initially, it will be tough and will have an opposite effect as you might end up slowing down. Trying to absorb more words at once that you used to may feel uncomfortable.

However, once your eye span manages to change and improve, you will find that your speed is going to rev up significantly.

You should also make use of hand movements for the sake of increasing your eye span. It has been seen that this movement increases the speed and eye span simultaneously. Using a pacer will surely help you absorb more words quickly. Later in this book (Chapter 3) I will show you a great exercise that increases both your reading speed and your eye span.

Keep Your Distance

Apart from this, you should make it a point to distance yourself from the text that you are reading. When you have a book located too close, your eye span is going to be fixated to a small region.

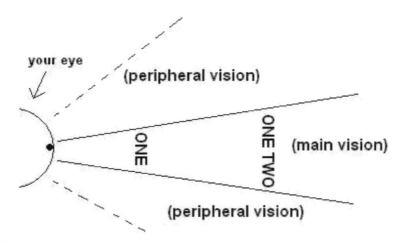

OK, once I have absolutely impressed you with my almighty and elite *MS Paint* skills, we can proceed further. It might be not the best detailed picture out there, but hey, you can get the idea.

What's interesting, when reading from a bigger distance, your eyes don't have to move that much to read a single line, so you will be more effective. In the beginning, try to increase the distance just a little bit – a few inches. If you are absolutely comfortable with it, you can increase it more. Remember that the distance will have to be adjusted every single time, depending on the light, font etc.

When you are reading the texts on a computer, you should follow the ergonomics and space yourself from the desk.

Now, let's talk about specific exercises that you should utilize. Sticking to them, not only will you make your eye muscles stronger, but also more flexible, while significantly slowing down the natural sight degradation that comes with aging.

Exercise A

This exercise will strengthen muscles inside your eye sockets, which will improve your peripheral vision and make your sight wider.

1. First of all, sitting or standing, hold both hands in front of you in a fist, palmed down. Now, extend your index fingers.

2. Pick a point right above your fingers and focus your sight on it. Now, start spreading your arms. You will see your fingers pass out of your foveal (main) vision. You'll feel the urge to follow them, but don't do it.

3. As you will move from the foveal to the peripheral, you will still see them, but you'll lose details.

4. Keep extending your arms until you reach the limit of your peripheral vision. Your fingers should stay at the very edge of your peripheral vision.

5. Without moving your head even a little bit and keeping your chin slightly raised, eyeball back and forth among right and left index fingers. You should just move your eyes. Do it ten times.

6. Repeat steps 1-5 three times.

Exercise B

This is an eye relaxation technique and takes only about four minutes. It will provide both your eyes and your head with more blood and hence, more oxygen, which will improve their work. It consists of two phases.

In the first one, you need to draw in air calmly and deeply, while opening your mouth and your eyes as extensively as possible to stretch out your whole face.

In the second phase, you need to close your lips and eyes as hard as you can, while also tightening the muscles of you neck, jaws, face-whole head. Then you have to hold your breath for thirty seconds with your muscles still tight and then exhale. Once done, repeat these two phases five more times. Take a fifteen seconds break and then go through these two phases again five more times.

Exercise C

This one will help your eyes relax. Do this several times whenever you feel tired during your reading sessions. First of all, close your eyes, but not entirely. Then focus on controlling your eyelids, so that they are not quivering. Doing this, you are relieving your eyeballs. With your eyelids still nearly closed, look at any distant object in front of you. Your eyes should start vibrating now. Remain like this as long as you feel comfortable.

Eye Adjustments

When it comes to speed reading, your eye movements will always hold the highest significance. We all have different styles and behaviour so the ease with which people can grasp the lessons is going to differ. Thus, when you are learning the dynamics of speed reading, you should be flexible enough to allow your eye to slowly make the right adjustments as per the new reading speed.

This is different from eye span. It covers a lot more aspects. We are talking of points like:

1. The number of times you blink your eye.

2. The duration for which you can gaze at the computer screen or your physical hardbound copies of texts which you wish to read.

3. The number of words which you can see in a glance which effectively is the eye span.

4. The ease and fluency with which you can move your eye from one block of text to another.

5. The amount of strain that is caused to your eye when you fixate yourself to a text.

Don't Read Words Per Se

This is one of the most crucial techniques of speed reading. It is extremely important to ensure that you huddle words together and read them in blocks. When you are reading more than one word at a time and not following the logic of reading words per se, it is going to be much more helpful in improving the speed with which you read. One important point to be kept in mind is that this change of habit may impact your comprehensibility power at the start. Some people take time to grasp the meaning of the words and this is why reading more than one word at a go can initially decrease the ease with which they can understand the meaning.

The thing you need to do is keep practicing this lesson until you perfect the art. When you manage to do so, you will be able to jump over segment of words, read them together and improve your reading speed substantially.

Ideally, you should have a soft gaze when you are reading. If you have an extremely focused gaze and you are overly attentive, you are likely to read the text one word at a time. This is why you need to try and keep the book a little farther away. This will increase your eye span and offer you a soft gaze which can aid in speed reading.

In elementary school, you were told to read every single letter and then glue them into a word. Now, you don't have to do this anymore. You instantly understand every word just by having a microsecond glance at it. **Notice taht letrets dno't enve hvae to be pcaled corelrcty for yuo to undrestnad htier maneing!** You brain has been trained long enough to get it anyways – as I wrote before, it's looking exclusively for the meaning, not words. The same goes to sentences. You can easily comprehend more than half of a sentence or a few sentences at a time, you just need to train it.

Have you ever noticed that whenever you see a street sign or a banner, you can read and understand the whole text instantly, but when you're reading a book, you only read word by word? When you take a glance at a sign or a banner, your sight gets it without zooming and focusing fully. It's called "soft gaze". So you read just partially focused. On the other hand, when you're reading a text, your sight tends to zoom-in and focus on each word. If you want to read faster than three hundred fifty words per minute, you have to learn how to use soft gaze.

Anytime you spend more than ½ a second on a word, your eyes naturally zoom-in, but if you suddenly see a bunch of words for less than ½ a second, your sight remains unfocused and you can absorb numerous words at once. There are two methods that you can use to keep your sight unfocused – the first one is to read so quick that your sight doesn't have enough time to zoom in – however, this only comes with practice and over time. You are probably not experienced enough just yet to make use of this one. There's the second method tough – you can blink in the midst of your eye rests to reset your focus and improve your speed almost instantly. I will tell you about this method in a moment and we'll do a little experiment, but first, let me tell you what "eye fixations" are.

Eye Rests (The So Called "Eye Fixation")

Our eyes have tendency to regularly stop and "take breaks" while reading. Children do it practically on every single word, adults – not much better, really – although it may sound unbelievable, most people stop **four times** every single second. We start reading left to right, stop for a microsecond on a word, then start again. It's like a train that should be an inter-city express, but stops in every single village – won't get to its destination too fast. This habit really slows down your progress. Too many stops will make you feel tired and will irritate your eyes.

First of all, you should observe yourself anytime you read from now on, to be conscious of how often you tend to stop. Then try to cut down eye stops to three or four per line - or ideally - even less. Of course, in a difficult material like e.g. engineering book, you will have to make more stops. Eventually you should be able to keep your eyes going smoothly, letting your mind absorb the material on the line as you go fast.

Let me show you what exactly we are talking about here. Let's make a little experiment. I prepared two versions of the same text. It's an excerpt from the popular book "Robinson Crusoe" by Daniel Defoe. Please read it at the usual speed so that you can understand it and measure your time using a stopwatch:

In this distress, the wind still blowing very hard, one of our men early in the morning cried out, `Land!' and we had no sooner run out of the cabin to look out in hopes of seeing whereabouts in the world we were, but the ship struck upon a sand, and in a moment, her motion being so stopped, the sea broke over her in such a manner that we expected we should all have perished immediately, and we were immediately driven into our close quarters to shelter us from the very foam and spray of the sea. It is not easy for any one, who has not been in the like condition, to describe or conceive the consternation of men in such circumstances; we knew nothing where we were, or upon what land it was we were driven, whether an island or the main, whether inhabited or not inhabited; and as the rage of the wind was still great, though rather less than at first, we could not so much as hope to have the ship hold many minutes without breaking in pieces, unless the winds by a kind of miracle should turn immediately about. In a word, we sat looking upon one another, and expecting death every moment, and every man acting accordingly, as preparing for another world, for there was little or nothing more for us to do in this; that which was our present comfort, and all the comfort we had was, that contrary to our expectation the ship did not break yet, and that the master said the wind began to abate.

Once you are done reading, write down your time. Now, read the same text, divided into three parts and use a stopwatch to measure your reading time again:

In this distress, the wind still blowing very hard, one of our men
early in the morning cried out, `Land!' and we had no sooner run

out of the cabin to look out in hopes of seeing whereabouts in
the world we were, but the ship struck upon a sand, and in a
moment, her motion being so stopped, the sea broke over her in
such a manner that we expected we should all have perished
immediately, and we were immediately driven into our close quarters
to shelter us from the very foam and spray of the sea. It is not easy

for any one, who has not been in the like condition, to describe
or conceive the consternation of men in such circumstances;
we knew nothing where we were, or upon what land it was we
were driven, whether an island or the main, whether
inhabited or not inhabited; and as the rage of the wind was still
great, though rather less than at first, we could not so much as
hope to have the ship hold many minutes without breaking in
pieces, unless the winds by a kind of miracle should turn
immediately about. In a word, we sat looking upon one another,
and expecting death every moment, and every man acting
accordingly, as preparing for another world, for there was little or
nothing more for us to do in this; that which was our present
comfort, and all the comfort we had was, that contrary to our
expectation the ship did not break yet, and that the master
said the wind began to abate.

If you accomplished this little experiment correctly, you will notice that you were able to read the second text significantly quicker than the first one. That's because the second formatting (called "block reading") includes only three fixations per line. **You may have not noticed it yet, but when you are on the middle column, you can usually see and understand the meaning of both left**

and right column as well. That what's peripheral vision does. I will tell you more about it later in this book. In reality, you can absorb much more than your "central/foveal/main vision" sees.

OK, let me now tell you about how you can use blinking to start reading faster right now. Let's do another experiment.

Eye Blinking

I have prepared another text for you. It's a short excerpt of a kid's story from http://www.my-kids-corner.com/harryspet.html.

Please read the following paragraph, but stop your eyes **only on the bold and underlined letters. You should spend no more than three quarters of a second on each stop:**

Harry lon**ge**d for a pet of his own, a **pe**rfect pet. But he wa**nt**ed something a litt**le** different from the **us**ual pet. Rabbits and guin**ea** pigs were all very w**el**l, but lots of people **ha**d those. And goldfi**sh** he thought were just a **li**ttle bit ordinary. Wh**at** Harry wanted was **so**mething unusual. "**A** dog's the thing," said Harr**y's** dad. "One of tho**se** great big, lolloping **sh**aggy ones like Mr. Fe**rr**is has next door. You coul**d** take it for walks a**nd** teach it to sit up an**d** beg." But Harry didn'**t** want a dog like Mr. Ferris **ha**d. Harry wanted s**o**mething different.

While Ha**rry** was playing in the gard**en** one morning he **sa**w something move **am**ong the leaves. A **b**rown, prickly something. A **b**rown prickly some**th**ing that Harry felt **wo**uld make the perfe**ct** pet.

"Hello," **sa**id Harry to the little hedgeh**og**. "Have you come **to** play?"

Now, read the same text again, but blink in between fixation points.

Was it different? You should be able to read the text at least a few times faster doing so. Don't worry, you won't have to blink so many times indefinitely. As you practice, you will learn to read with soft gaze all the time, almost effortlessly.

Keywords and Selective Reading

Another important matter is that you should focus solely on the most important words in each sentence, while omitting the rest. To understand what I mean here, read the text again, but pay attention only to the bolded words:

Harry longed for a **pet** of his **own**, a **perfect** pet. But he **wanted** something a little **different from** the usual pet. **Rabbits** and **guinea pigs** were all very **well**, but **lots** of **people had** those. And **goldfish** he thought **were** just a little bit **ordinary**. What **Harry wanted** was something **unusual**. "**A dog's the thing**," said **Harry's dad**. "One of **those** great **big**, lolloping **shaggy** ones like **Mr. Ferris** has **next door**. You **could** take it for **walks** and **teach** it to **sit up** and **beg**." But Harry **didn't want a dog** like Mr. Ferris **had**. **Harry wanted** something **different**.

While Harry was **playing** in the **garden** one **morning** he saw **something** move **among the leaves**. A brown, **prickly** something. A brown prickly something that **Harry felt** would make **the perfect pet**.

"Hello," **said Harry** to the **little hedgehog**. "Have you **come** to **play?**"

Yes - you can still get the unimportant words, without even focusing and looking right at them. That's your peripheral vision working here as well. These words are not crucial to the meaning, so you brain can absorb them by just simply overpassing them. This kind of reading will improve both your speed and comprehension. Of course it will be harder as the words won't be bolded, but here is a simple rule that can help you: your brain doesn't really need *at, in, a, but, an, I, me, the, etc.* and other short words (< three letters) to understand the meaning. Some other words are often just fillers too, irrelevant for the meaning. Focusing on the crucial words is much more effective and not so tiring for your mind. Anytime you read, focus just on the most important words. Like everything else, it takes practice, but it's a great strategy.

More About Your Peripheral Vision

You can train your brain to take in much larger loads of information, just like you can train your muscles in the gym to make them stronger and more durable. You can take a random book now and open it on a random page. Look at it just for one second and then close it. Do you think that you could recognize this very page later? Yes, you could. We all have the ability of photographic memory, but it has to be trained and taken care of. Think about how many details you can memorize walking down the street, on a gas station or anywhere else - so often just by taking a microsecond glance at the whole place. There's a good exercise that you can use to improve your peripheral vision:

1. Take an article or a book, it can also be a blog post.

2. Don't read from left to right, but imagine that there's a red line right down the middle, e.g.

> Midland Transit Service is a small municipal transit
> system in the Town of Midland, in Simcoe County,
> Ontario, Canada. Two routes operate from the hub
> at King and Elizabeth Streets every half-hour on
> weekdays and every hour on Saturday,
> with no service on Sundays and holidays.
> Midland also offers a wheelchair accessible van service,
> operated by *Community Link North Simcoe*, that offers
> door to door service. The bus depot and public works
> maintenance facility is located at 731 Ontario Street,
> but the system is administered from
> the town offices at 575 Dominion Avenue.

(It's just a random article from Wikipedia to show you what I'm talking about, you should use longer texts though.)

3. At the beginning, you can try to just "absorb" the left or the right side when going down. You should also use your finger to attract your attention to the imaginary line.

4. Practicing more, you should train your mind to see both sides when your sight is focused on the line in the center. Don't get frustrated as it may be really difficult at the beginning (like almost everything, right?). It's an advanced technique, but you should be aware that this kind of reading is possible and you should practice it until it comes with no effort. Advanced speed readers are able to see and understand lines consisting of 8-10 words (or more) at a single glance.

More Peripheral Vision Exercises

These exercises may help you in mastering your peripheral vision. You should practice them once a day as long as you can see the results.

Exercise A

Sit at a desk or a table, so that your eyes are on the same level. Just in front of you, at the distance of your arms, place any objects that you will be focusing your sight on. Then, take several varied objects and put them in the area of your peripheral vision, distanced differently. While still focusing on the central object, try to notice the details of all these things lying in the area of your peripheral vision. With more practice, you will be able to recognize many details with less endeavor, as you brain will become trained to make use of your peripheral vision.

Exercise B

For this one, you will need a friend or some other kind of assistant. Find single colored wall and face it, at the length of your extended arms. Tape a photo, picture or anything that you can focus on to the wall. It has to be in your main field of vision. Now ask your friend to move different objects in diverse paces below and above your field of vision. While still focusing on the object taped to the wall, try to recognize these objects. You can also start with colored shapes to make it easier for the beginning, and then proceed to different objects.

Instead of doing the exercise B with a friend, you can tape different objects to a wall, then proceed like in the exercise A. That will be different though, as the moving objects train your vision differently. You can also do exercise A with someone else, who will slide one object at a time on the table. Once you get the idea, you can make changes. You should do one of these two every day and then immediately proceed to the "red line" text exercise.

You can also exercise your peripheral vision when working or playing on your computer. While still looking at your screen, from time to time pay attention to the areas around it – objects on the wall, loudspeakers, your window etc. You can also move your hands in the area of your peripheral vision to notice the motion and details.

Mind you that whenever you have a headache, you need to stop your exercises. They should not be painful at all. It's no gym weight training.

Improve your Knowledge Base

Now, you might be wondering as to how is this directly connected with the dynamics of speed reading. However, when you look closely, you will find that it definitely has a lot to do with your speed. Try reading a text that has nothing to do with the genres of article you are familiar with. For instance, if you are a medical scholar, take up core accounting articles and vice versa. When you are reading such texts, you will find that your reading speed is going to drop down considerably. This is because you are reading something that is beyond your knowledge base.

Not only this - even when you are reading a text and you come across complex jargons or words that you don't know and are therefore hard to spell, you may find it extremely hard to read the texts at high speed. This is the reason you need to improve your knowledge base. Try and venture into articles on almost all possible genres as this will prepare you to read all types of texts without any speed break. At the same time, you are expected to improve your vocabulary as well because it will be a befitting way of handling the complex words that are likely to be found in texts and articles. Of course, you can't be an expert in everything, but the more you know, the less fixations you will have on each line and a faster reader you will become.

Speed Reading Software

You must have heard of software that can help you in speed reading. There are many variations that you can find and each of them is going to offer you something that can improve your skills.

You can find software that keeps blasting the words on your screen. You will have the option of choosing the speed which you want. Ideally, you should start from a slow speed as it will help you get familiar with the interface. Once it has happened, you can then slowly increment the speed in small busts and try the maximum speed at which you can read. Consecutive words coming on to your screen at extremely quick speed from two different sides will increase both your eye span and attentiveness. Some of these programs will have lines roll up automatically. The speed with which the lines keep on rolling will vary. It will start slowly and subsequently, then it will become extremely fast.

Most of the time, you will find that this type of software also comes up with some questions at the end. The questions are not usually going to be extremely analytical, they merely serve to test whether or not you paid heed to the lessons that you read when you were concentrating on increasing your speed. These questions will give you an idea of your comprehension level and progress. Moreover, you will be able to measure and write down your progress more accurately.

Ideally, if you have chosen a paid software, you should go through the trial version and examine if you are comfortable using it.

If you are not willing to spend extra money for this, you can always opt for free tools.

Rapid Serial Visual Presentation

This remains by far one of the best techniques that is in extensive use. The main idea behind this technique is to offer you a single word to read at the start. As there is only one word on the screen at a time, your attention is less likely to be diverted. However, as the time progresses, you can control the speed with which the words keep popping. There is no guarantee that the words will pop on the same place in your screen and thus your eye span, concentration, attentiveness and need to grasp the word will be put to test. While the words will be flashed and the speed will increase extensively, you may find yourself reading an impressive amount of words together.

Most speed reading software makes use of this technique as it's very effective. Once your eyes will get adjusted to words being popped at a tremendous speed on your screen, you will start seeing progress.

But again, as it's very important, so let me repeat myself here: when you are reading a text, you should devote your undivided attention to it and read words without vocalizing them, even in the back of your mind.

Now I'm going to show you two cool free websites where you can practice your speed reading almost effortlessly:

http://www.accelareader.com – just copy and paste the text that you want to read and there you go. In "settings" section, you can adjust reading speed and play with a few other options. As soon as you get comfortable with higher speeds, you should start widening "chink size" – by doing this you will condition your brain to read several words (or sentences) at a time, which will highly increase your reading speed and improve your eye fixation over time. Not only is this a perfect website for exercising daily, but also a great time saver for the times you have to read lengthy articles on your computer. I won't give you links here, but I'm quite sure that you can easily find similar applications for your smart phones.

http://www.tools4noobs.com/summarize/ - this interesting tool will save your time by cutting out all the unnecessary fluff from a text, preparing you a nice summary. You can also mess around with a few options there. Of course, it's not always working perfectly fine – it depends on the structure of each article - so I wouldn't be euphoric about it, but still – it may prove helpful, and without any doubts, it's an interesting website.

Basically, these are the main techniques, strategies and ideas which you need to follow. An important point that you need to keep in mind is that different people have varying capabilities. You have to analyze your own strengths and weaknesses and be aware of the ways and methods that can create in a larger difference for you.

You can choose a mix and mash of all these methods and after you are sure that you are making substantial progress, you can then keep trying these strategies until you have perfected the art of speed reading.

Chapter 4: The Habits That Will Help You Become A Speed Reader (+More Practical Exercises)

Speed reading is more than just techniques. There are plenty of other details which you need to know as well. If you want to perfect the art of speed reading, you have to keep some other points in mind. In this chapter, I will talk about some of the tips, exercises and general precautions which you need to bear in mind. With these points checked, it will be easier for you to concentrate on these aspects and thus the odds of making significant inroads into speed reading will be much better.

Charge Your Eyes

Here's another simple exercise that you can try right now. You should ideally do it before every reading session. You don't have to go back to this very picture all the time, you can just redraw it using a marker or print it (you can make it bigger). For twenty seconds, follow the line as fast as you can. **Don't move your head, just your eyeballs:**

Instead, you can also look on the wall and imagine that you're writing your first and last name on it using your sight. The point here is to move your eyeballs rapidly in patterns for an extended amount of time.

Now, here's what you do next: grab a pacer, move it under the sentences in your book and let it guide your sight. Read using all the ideas and strategies mentioned earlier in this book. Keep going faster and faster under you've reached your limit. Now slow down a little bit (let's say, five to ten percent). Voila, here's your new reading speed!

You should also "charge" your eyes with this picture before your **Deadline** exercises.

Deadline Strategy

Now I'm going to show you two practical exercises/habits that you should really stick to if you want to increase your speed. Remember that you will practice them not to read, but to solely increase your speed, your "glancing" at words and pacer-to-eye coordination – just like a boxer is not practicing his left hook while he's stretching or lifting weights.

Measure how long does it take you to read one page of text and then try to meet or beat that time. Do it whenever you read anything. Now, for every next page that should contain similar amount of text, try to read a little bit faster. You should treat it like a funny competition with yourself. Since it's an exercise, your comprehension may decrease a little while doing it, but the main focus here is to increase your speed - you have to be faster than you normally read. You must go out of your comfort zone of how fast are you used to normally read, and rewire your brain, step by step. Don't worry about your understanding here. It can feel slightly unnatural at the beginning, but this impression will change over time. That's the point. It's really nice when you notice that you read a page faster than the previous one, even if it's just, say, four seconds. Constantly try to go faster.

You will also have to practice this exercise – definitely THE BEST ONE, and probably the only one in a long run that will increase your speed and your peripheral vision tremendously:

1. Take an article (two A4 pages should do, can be longer though) and read it for ten minutes (set a timer) at your normal, average speed. Mark where you ended reading.

2. Now, go back to the beginning and read the same article again, but do it faster- in six or seven minutes. The goal here is to get used to seeing words while going fast. **Don't forget to use your hand, pen or other pacer.**

3. When the timer rings, go back again and now tell yourself that you will read the text in just five minutes. Again, it will be hard to understand completely everything, but that's not the point.

4. Now, for the last time - repeat the cycle again, but now you'll have to go through the text in only four minutes.

5. Congratulations! You just completed your first speed reading training! Now – find yourself a new article. Make sure it's on a similar level when it comes to difficulty – read it for one minute and this time read normally, don't rush. Once done, measure your reading speed. There's a huge possibility of you noticing an improvement. If your speed is still the same- have no fear! :-) - you will get there!

6. Deadlines help you focus. **Do this effective exercise for three weeks, fifteen minutes a day.**

Hey, There's More!

As soon as you feel that you are fluent with reading at speed (it may take you three weeks or longer) you can proceed to more advanced exercises.

These techniques will improve your peripheral reading, skimming skills and speed. Comprehension will come over time as you stick to your training.

Let me now shock you again with my extravagant artistic skills.

Sweeping Every Second Line:

Ratcliff was the son of Robert Ratcliff and his wife Emily. His father was a brewer in th~~partnership of Bass Ratcliff and Gretton and lived at Newton Solney in south Derbyshire. H~~ was educated at Rossall School and Cambridge University. ~~Ratcliff followed his father in~~ ~~the brewery and was also an~~ active member of the territorial reserve. He was commissione into the 2nd Volunteer Battalion of the 5th Staffordshire ~~Rifle Volunteer Corps~~ on 19 Marc 1887, as a ~~Second Lieutenant serving~~ with "B" Company at Burton. He was promoted t Lieutenant on 27 July 1889, Captain on 23 January 1892, ~~and Major 9 July 1900.~~

In 1900 Ratcliff ~~was elected~~ as Liberal Unionist Member of Parliament for Burton. With th reformation of the Territorial reserves he became Honorary ~~Lieutenant-Colonel of th~~ 6th North ~~Staffordshire Regiment~~ on 21 September 1907 and succeeded John Gretton a Lieutenant-Colonel in command of the 6th North Staffords on 18 November 1909.

This kind of reading/sweeping is very similar to normal reading, but here you need to force your eyes to absorb two lines of text at a time.

You will get the best results reading at a high pace. Again, you need to measure your reading time and write down your progression in a notebook. Remember – first of all you might find yourself forgetting most of the information even before you finish reading a paragraph but:

1. Your comprehension will rise over time. Patience and perseverance = key.

2. The point here is to get used to using your peripheral vision, skimming, reading fast, pacing and all the other techniques at one shot.

3. You should be doing this exercise before your reading sessions – it will help you warm-up your eye muscles, will improve your starting speed and help you in many other aspects.

After you get used to this kind of sweeping, you can try absorbing more lines at once:

Ratcliff was the son of Robert Ratcliff and his wife Emily. His father was a brewer in the partnership of Bass Ratcliff and Gretton and lived at Newton Solney in south Derbyshire. He was educated at Rossall School and Cambridge University. Ratcliff followed his father into the brewery and was also an active member of the territorial reserve. He was commissioned into the 2nd Volunteer Battalion of the 5th Staffordshire Rifle Volunteer Corps on 19 March 1887, as a Second-Lieutenant serving with "B" Company at Burton. He was promoted to Lieutenant on 27 July 1889, Captain on 23 January 1892, and Major 18 July 1900.

In 1900 Ratcliff was elected as Liberal Unionist Member of Parliament for Burton. With the reformation of the Territorial reserves he became Honorary Lieutenant-Colonel of the 6th North Staffordshire Regiment on 21 September 1907 and succeeded John Gretton as Lieutenant-Colonel in command of the 6th North Staffords on 18 November 1909.

Eventually, you should be able to read a few lines at once, but starting from the back:

Ratcliff was the son of Robert Ratcliff and his wife Emily. His father was a brewer in the partnership of Bass Ratcliff and Gretton and lived at Newton Solney in south Derbyshire. He was educated at Rossall School and Cambridge University. Ratcliff followed his father into the brewery and was also an active member of the territorial reserve. He was commissioned into the 2nd Volunteer Battalion of the 5th Staffordshire Rifle Volunteer Corps on 19 March 1887, as a Second-Lieutenant serving with "B" Company at Burton. He was promoted to Lieutenant on 27 July 1889, Captain on 23 January 1892, and Major 18 July 1900.

In 1900 Ratcliff was elected as Liberal Unionist Member of Parliament for Burton. With the reformation of the Territorial reserves he became Honorary Lieutenant-Colonel of the 6th North Staffordshire Regiment on 21 September 1907 and succeeded John Gretton as Lieutenant-Colonel in command of the 6th North Staffords on 18 November 1909.

I know how unreal it might sound to you, but it's absolutely possible and much easier than you think. Remember- we all have our photographic memory already "installed". It just needs a little training. When reading from the back, you just keep all the information in your memory until you reach the beginning of the last sentence – that's when all the data starts "clicking". This way you can read and skim at the same time. You should also practice this before your actual reading, as an exercise.

Summarization Habit

This is habit is obligatory if you want to be an effective reader and quick learner. Here's what you do when reading and after you finish reading your material, step-by-step:

Reading:

1. You should always be a dynamic reader (always ask the questions I told you about in the earlier chapters, know why are you reading etc.).

2. You should skim and look for golden nuggets – a book is a knowledge mine, but you can't waste your time digging where there is no gold, just ordinary rocks that you don't need.

3. Make mental reminders using association/imagination technique (Bee-Gees dancing on a chess board!).

Summarizing:

1. Make a simple summary of what you just read- it should consist of intro, body, and conclusion. You can also write it down. Use your own words if possible.

2. Prepare a set of questions about the material and try to answer them in your head. Try to imagine possible exam questions. Be your own exam after you finish your reading session.

Also ask yourself these questions:

1. Do I comprehend what I just read, how much of the material do I remember?

2. Did I retain at least seventy % of the text?

After all this, you should skim the material three more times – read again all the areas that you didn't comprehend (go back to the marks you made), including headings etc. If you need to memorize anything, do it right then using the imagination-association techniques.

Practice Your Lessons Periodically

Speed reading isn't a habit that you can hope to develop overnight. If you are serious about self-development, you need to be sure that you are diligently practicing the exercises. One reason a lot of us fail to make the cut is because we take it leisurely. You need to understand that your speed reading self-classes should be held regularly. You have to make a timetable and stick to it. There are no shortcuts and no one will do the work for you.

You should use a blend of these strategies. Ideally, opt for a mix up of all these methods so that you can make the most out of it. However, do not miss out on practicing them even for a single day because it can hamper the flow. When you are a novice, you will keep making progress every single day. You are actually training your mind to fall in a different loop when you are reading and if you do not practice it with the needed levels of dedication, disciplining your mind in the new habit can be a lot tougher than what you have imagined.

So, make a plan and then ensure that you are following it diligently. Do not be lazy with the plan because even a single day of missed routines may have a negative impact on your learning habit and demotivate you.

Paid Speed Reading Programs

There are also specific programs and training courses that you can choose to enrol for. When you are a part of these programs, they will follow a systematic pattern where you will be taught the right strategies which you must implement in a systematic and organized manner. These programs should keep the needs of different readers in mind. You shouldn't be expecting miracles though – the strategies and techniques used to master the art of speed reading are pretty much the same. If you want to give it a shot, always try to find someone who had finished the program to ensure that you won't spend your money and time (some of the courses can be long and expensive) on some wishy-washy obvious small-talk between teachers and students.

We all have different needs and requirements, at the same time; the ease with which people can grasp the lessons is going to differ as well. Thus, the speed reading coaching should be flexible enough to allow readers to adjust their own reading speed and ease with which the program can be put to use.

Most of the programs will offer you instructions that can help you carry out the same strategies at home. When you want to make the most out of them, discipline and dedication remain two of the most sought characteristics. You need to follow a disciplined attitude and you must be dedicated enough to follow the program till the very end. The cool feature here is that you will have your course-mates that will keep you motivated as you will be probably competing a bit and comparing your progress.

What Are Your Sleeping Patterns?

Your sleeping patterns tell a lot about your results. They have an impact on how you carry out your tasks and various other aspects of your life as well.

If you are interested in speed reading, it is important to be mindful of your sleeping cycles. We have discussed the techniques and you must by now be well aware of the need to be attentive. If you do not sleep well, your focus and attentiveness will suffer and this isn't the kind of situation you want to be in.

Some of us are able to get a good sleep everyday regardless of the situation and stress you may be suffering from. However, there are a lot of us who are unable to rest completely and in such cases; lack of ample sleep can turn out to be troublesome for the sake of enhancing your speed of reading.

If you are unable to enjoy peaceful sleep, you can choose techniques like meditation and yoga. Both these methods are extremely helpful in bringing about a feeling of calmness and relaxation. When you are calm and relaxed, you are much more likely to fall asleep.

Lack of sleep leads to stress and when you are stressed out, you will find it hard to concentrate on the reading exercise. A minimum of 6 hours of sleep every day is recommended for smooth working of your body.

Try and read articles only when you feel refreshed and energetic and at that time, record your reading speed. You will find that your speed is sure to pick up as compared to the times when you are lethargic and tired owing to lack of ample rest.

You may have heard about it already lots of times, but it's very important to wake up in the morning. I usually begin my day at 5 A.M. The fresh feeling and energy that waking up before everyone and starting another productive day gives me is just priceless. It may be difficult to change your sleeping habits, but believe me – going to sleep early and waking up in the morning is definitely worth it. You should get the most of your work done before noon.

If you don't believe me and you think that I sound just like your grumpy aunt, then ask uncle Google about sleeping patterns of the most successful, richest, remarkable and powerful people on this planet. The early bird gets the worm.

The Right Food

Now you may be wondering as to what is the relation between your diet and speed reading. But if you examine things at the root of the matter; everything is related to each other. Your food patterns and eating habit will have significance on the speed with which you can read the texts and learn. The main reason is that it is a healthy diet that leads to a healthy body.

When you are eating the right food that stimulates your brain, your attention span will really improve. Think of yourself running a race where you have to come first as being second is not an option for you. Time will definitely be an extremely important factor. Now to clinch the race, you would need a blend of the following:

Attentiveness: you have to be attentive so that you do not end up losing even a single second of your allotted time. The slightest recklessness and lack of concentration on your part may end up costing you victory.

Speed: you need to be agile because every second counts. The higher the speed, the better will be your chance of clinching the game.

Health: can you ever win a race if you are not physically healthy? Imagine yourself running really fast and falling on the race track because you are unfit to run the full length of the course.

All three of these points are applicable even in your task of speed reading. Imagine yourself reading the paragraphs with a sloppy attentiveness. You are most likely to go through the same paragraph over and over again because you will not be able to grasp the content. If you are not taking good care of your heath, your overall speed will come down.

This is what brings us to need to stick to a healthy diet. You can find food and beverages that act as stimulants e.g. **dark chocolate (unsweetened!), honey, agave syrup, ginseng, guarana, gotu kola, coconut oil, cacao powder, cayenne pepper, ginger or chia seeds.** They will be helpful when you are looking to stay alert or active. On the other hand, you should avoid caffeine. You might be convinced that your cup of coffee is helping you, but not really. Your attention levels are spiking just for a very short time, just to take a nose-dive later – then you end up even more tired, disturbed and irritated.

The best brain-foods include **oily fish (e.g. salmon, herring), all kinds of nuts, blueberries, tomatoes, seeds, blackcurrants, broccoli, sage, avocados and whole grains**. You should also make sure that you don't have any **allergies or gluten intolerance**. They can be fatal to your concentration and overall well-being.

If you want to know more about the so called brain-food, there is a comprehensive book by Mark Hyman M.D, "The UltraMind Solution" that I can recommend.

Stay Hydrated! Stay Hydrated! Stay Hydrated!

<u>This can't be told enough</u>. You HAVE TO stay hydrated. When your body lacks the right water balance, it can be troublesome for your health and just deadly for your concentration. When your body has the perfect water balance, you are going to focus much easier and have improved attention.

When your body is not hydrated, your pupils will not be able to function properly. Lack of proper eyesight is going to hamper the speed with which you are reading the texts. Your focus will also be deeply decreased and frequent headaches are also possible. This is why water is extremely important. So, be sure that you drink enough water and keep your body hydrated. You should start every day with a glass (or two) of **plain mineral water**, and drink eight 8-ounce glasses of water a day (~ 2 liters). Don't substitute plain mineral water with soda, coke, sweet juices, black tea or anything else at all! It's **v-e-r-y** <u>important for your speed reading progress and your overall health!</u> If you don't like the taste of plain mineral water, you can also try preparing your own <u>fruit-infused water.</u>

Stay Stress Free

While speed reading is a healthy habit, remember, it is not the most mandatory thing ever. It is always an advantage to have the ability to speed read as you can grasp a matter in quick time, but while you should be passionate about excelling in this field, you should also make it a point not to overdo it. Doing so is only going to lead to stress.

Whenever you have a hobby or a passion, you have to invest positive energy in it. You should never commit the mistake of being overzealous to an extent that it becomes an addiction. In such cases, even the slightest failure can lead to stress which in turn will hamper the progress you might have already made.

Stress is going to act as a speed breaker and will be a serious limiting factor for you. You need to overcome the problems and the best way to achieve excellence in any field is to love it and be passionate about it. Do not be obsessed with the habit and be happy with whatever progress you are making. Over a period of time, it is definitely going to show you some positive results. Being stressed about a situation is never going to reap you positive benefits, and this is one reason as to why you need to be sure that you know how to keep your calm.

Being generally stress-free in your life will also help you concentrate, sleep better, feel better and eat better, which in turn will start an upward spiral of well-being. Meditation is precisely what I do to achieve it. Not only does it allow me to feel better every day and be focused like a laser beam on my personal goals, but also helps me in my speed reading sessions. I have also written a book on everyday meditation. It's selling very well in the UK & in the US, and I think that it's really decent. If you're interested, you can find it and grab it here:

http://tinyurl.com/meditationbeginnersguide

Another great habit that can help you is to manage stress making use of neuro-linguistic programming and mindfulness. If you feel like it might be a good solution for you, you can read my book called **"Mindfulness Based Stress and Anxiety Management Tools"**:

http://www.mindfulnessforsuccess.com/positive-psychology-coaching/giveaway.html

Read, Read More and Read Again

The best possible tip you can use for speed reading is to keep reading more. The more you read, the better. Whenever you are reading a lot of articles and you have covered different topics, it is going to help you expand your knowledge horizon and your dictionary. When you are looking to improve your speed of reading, you need to have a broad horizon of knowledge. When you read something that falls in your ground of familiar territory, you are going to preview it faster and at the same time, skimming through it and reading it is going to be a pleasure for you.

We all have our own comfort zone that we love. Whenever we read articles which are in genres that we feel relaxed in, it is going to be much easier for us to speed read. However, when you chart into an unknown territory, your brain is going to take longer to process the information and comprehending the text along with reading it speedily can be a cumbersome task. This is why you need to expand your comfort zone. The more you read, the more you will be familiar with the different topics and areas. This is going to help you in improving your speed reading capabilities.

While you can read more to improve your reading horizon, you must be aware of the fact that it is not possible to encompass all fields. We all have our own specific areas of interest that we are more comfortable in. This is why you need to understand that not all texts are meant to be read at tremendous speed.

Also remember that it is sometimes okay to just lay back and enjoy a piece of text rather than focus solely on reading it at an extremely high speed. Reading is an activity which is meant to be enjoyed thoroughly. So, you should make it a point to read as much as possible. Not only will it help you in speed reading, it will also help you in life, in general.

Time Your Lessons

It might look irritating initially, but you should always remember to time your lessons. If you are really looking forward to ace your speed reading skills, you ought to set a timer on your table, every time you read. Make sure to follow a disciplined approach here. Turn it on exactly before start and put it off right after finish. At the same time, be diligent about this habit and do not carry it out as per will.

When you are following it in a systemic manner, you will be able to spot the pattern. Sometimes, it may so happen that your words read per minute might fall down. These are the times when you need to get a grip over the different ways you may be going wrong and try your lessons all over again.

Keep a Track of Your Progress

Along with a timer, you need to maintain a journal wherein you will record this data which will reflect the progress which you have been making. As you keep following the points and methods, you will find the changes begin to show.

Some people just use these different methods randomly without paying any heed to the kind of advantages they have been reaping. Do not use this haywire wayward approach as it is important to have a record of what you have done and how far you have progressed. When you manage to make the right calculations, it will give you an insight into the lessons that have been the most useful.

Each one of us has different personality and thus the methods which have helped me improve my reading speed might not help you equally. This is why you have to keep track of your progress. Doing this will help you in sketching a rough idea as to which methods are of help and whether you need some change of strategies.

There are various ways by which you can increase your speed and if a certain style doesn't suit you, you can always opt for a change of method. Those who fail to keep a track of the changes will never know if they have made any significant progress and thus they might keep practicing ways that will ultimately lead them to nowhere.

You can also choose software that helps you measure your reading speed and save the results, and this is one of the best indicators of how efficiently you are progressing. With such efficient tools, it will be a whole lot easier for you to analyze the improvements you are making. If you fail to spot any significant change, the best thing you could do is make a change of your routine and you can try to do things a little differently.

One important point to be remembered here is that if your reading speed shows variable patterns as it rises and falls and there is no steady movement as such, do not be disappointed. The rise and fall of reading speed is an extremely common scenario. It mainly happens because of the content of the text. The lack of interest and passion in the topic is going to impact the kind of reading speed which you will have. Do not get disappointed by such haphazard movements in your progress graph.

Remember, you need to be committed and dedicated to your passion for speed reading. Keep an eye on the progress meter and try and come up with ways by which you can improve further.

These are the key points which you should keep in mind. Speed reading is a habit that may develop over a period of time. When you have managed to grasp this habit, it will start coming naturally to you.

The more you try it, the better you are going to get at it. You can obviously have your own unique set of tips that you need to follow and ideally, all you need to do is have a systematic plan that you must keep in mind. Planning successive steps and aiming high is the key recipe to attaining your goals.

Take Breaks & Reward Yourself

It's not a secret that reading hour by hour with no stops is going to decrease your effectively. Both your body and your mind need regular breaks. A good idea might be to set goals, and then reward yourself for achieving them. For example, you can tell yourself that you will read one hundred pages in the next sixty minutes and set an alarm. Then reward yourself with a tasty sandwich or a delicious dried fruit when you've achieved your goal. You should ideally divide the reading time of one hour by three, and after twenty minutes you ought to take four to five minutes breaks during which you should take a walk or move your body to provide it with more oxygen and avoid back pains etc. **Don't use these breaks to watch movies on YouTube or TV** or for some other dull activity, it will just have an opposite effect!

Chapter 5: Do Not Give Up

How far have you truly progressed? If your progress has been remarkable, you are on track to completely excel in this form of reading. However, if the progress hasn't been so exceptional and you are still stuck at slow reading speed, you might be wondering if all these methods are really going to bring a change?

This is one of the trickiest phases, as a lot of people end up being demotivated. When you feel like giving up because you have lost faith in the program, you need to get yourself together. Don't lose when you're already in the wining position. Do not fall down before the last hill, soldier! There are various ways by which you can stay motivated and focused. Here, let's talk about some of these.

- **Everyone is Unique**

Never compare your progress with someone else. It is an absolutely ridiculous thing to do. While there are people who are naturally gifted when it comes to fast reading, there is no reason as to why you cannot develop this habit. I coached many students on my university and everyone who hadn't surrendered succeeded. **The only person you should compare your progress to is yourself.** Further, being a slow reader is not a crime. Obviously, when you can read something fast, it can be of help in various ways. However, this doesn't means that slow readers need to be haunted by an inferiority complex.

The ease with one is learning the lessons and the time of progress is going to vary. **It doesn't matter how long you are going to take to excel in this skill. All that matters is that you will get there eventually and the only thing that remains important is whether or not you can clinch to the final goal.** If you manage to actually spot signs of improvement in your reading speed, it will definitely help you out.

So, do not let any kind of inferiority complex haunt you. It is this inferiority which often leads to killing of hope and this is not the situation you would like to be stuck in.

- **Hold On to Hope, You WILL Do It!**

When you are sure that things WILL work your way, it gives you the confidence to keep going ahead. Hope is an extremely strong emotion that is sure to reap the best dividends for you and believing in yourself is crucial to your inner game and success. This is one of the strongest ways by which you can make a befitting difference. When you feel like giving up on all the lessons, remember that it is the hope to succeed that has paved the path for success. When others could do it, even the slowest readers and learners, there is nothing that will prevent you from achieving the same. So, why should you give up now after having invested so much time and effort in the lessons and activities?

When you dream of better tidings and you know that you WILL do it, they are sure to come long. If you have read about the law of attraction, you would already be aware of the fact that it states that the events that occur around us are a direct manifestation of the thoughts that swirl in our mind.

If you are a firm believer of this theory, you know the importance of clinging on to hope and believing that no matter how tiring and slow the journey may be; it will take you to your goals if you keep **TAKING ACTION.** You should never give up. There may be times and situations when things look gloomy and it is natural to be disappointed. However, this does not mean that you should leave the race and call it quits. Just give it one more push and it might end up making all the difference that you had ever needed.

- **Nothing is Impossible**

It is absolutely ridiculous to even believe that anything is impossible. If you feel like giving up because you do not have the right results in front of you, ask one question to yourself; "what is preventing you from succeeding?" In this question, you will get the key to your own dilemma. There has to be some sort of reason. It could be the fear of failure, the inability to concentrate, the lack of passion, the absence of dedication, poor diet, dehydration, lack of sleep and so many other reasons as well. When you are trying to understand your own flaws and the areas you have gone wrong, you will be able to get an insight into the ways by which you can rectify the mistakes.

There is absolutely nothing in this world which was made to be unachievable, by which I mean that if there is someone who could do it, you can probably accomplish the same too. If you want to earn one hundred billion dollars by selling socks on eBay in the next two weeks, that might be quite impossible and you need to start setting your goals realistically, but speed reading is easier than you think and possible for everyone who is literate at all. Sure, it can take a long time and it might test your patience once in a while, but as long as you are sure that you are going to work it out, you will reach your destination.

You have all the tips and strategies with you. You do not need to hunt down ways by which you can make it work. All you need is a disciplined attitude that can truly make it real.

These are the general tips that you need to follow. Remember, a lot of games need you to have a mental edge. When you lose the challenge in your mind, even the best words of wisdom will not be able to make it work for you. So, keep working till the very end and the results will definitely appear, and you WILL become a speed reader.

Conclusion

Speed reading is achievable for everyone. If I could do it, you can too. Now, with all these ideas, strategies, techniques and exercises I gave you, you should put your shoulder to the wheel – go for it and you won't be sorry! The best time to start is always NOW. There's no point at all in reading anything if you are not willing to make the use of the knowledge. Just pick one of the techniques or exercises I gave you and try it **right now.** Then buy a notebook, plan your sessions and **officially start your training.** This world is full of books that can make your life **easier and happier,** but if you want to assimilate all the knowledge, you need to **take action**. Don't wait any more, don't waste your time – **start you journey today,** help yourself and be successful!

<u>One last thing before you go – Can I ask you a favor? I need your help!</u> If you like this book, could you please share your experience <u>HERE</u> on Amazon and write an honest review? It will be just one minute for you (I will be happy even with one sentence!), but a GREAT help for me. Here's the direct link: https://goo.gl/mck4cY Since I'm not a well-established author and I don't have powerful people and big publishing companies supporting me, <u>I read every single review and jump around with joy like a little kid every time my readers comment on my books and give me their honest feedback!</u> If I was able to inspire you in any way, please let me know! It will also help me get my books in front of more people looking for new ideas and useful knowledge. If you did not enjoy the book or had a problem with it, please don't hesitate to contact me at contact@mindfulnessforsuccess.com and tell me how I can improve it to provide more value and more knowledge to my readers. I'm constantly working on my books to make them better and more helpful. Thank you and good luck! I believe in you and wish you all the best on your new journey!

Your friend,
Ian

My Free Gift to You
Discover How to Get Rid of Stress & Anxiety and Reach Inner Peace in 20 Days or Less!

To help speed up your personal transformation, I have prepared a special gift for you!

Download my full, 120 page e-book "Mindfulness Based Stress and Anxiety Management Tools" (Value: $9.99) for free by clicking here.

Moreover, by becoming my subscriber, you will be the first one to **get my new books for only $0.99,** during their short two day promotional launch. **I passionately write about**: social dynamics, career, Neuro-Linguistic Programming, goal achieving, positive psychology and philosophy, life hacking, meditation and becoming the most awesome version of yourself. Additionally, once a week I will send you insightful tips and **free e-book offers** to keep you on track on your journey to becoming the best you!

That's my way of saying **"thank you"** to my new and established readers and helping you grow. I hate spam and e-mails that come too frequently – **you will never receive more than one email a week! Guaranteed.**

Just follow this link:
http://www.mindfulnessforsuccess.com/positive-psychology-coaching/giveaway.html

Hey there like-minded friends, let's get connected!

Don't hesitate to visit:

-My blog: www.mindfulnessforsuccess.com

-My facebook fanpage: https://www.facebook.com/mindfulnessforsuccess

-My twitter: https://twitter.com/mindfulness78

Twitter handle: @Mindfulness4Success
-My Instagram profile: https://instagram.com/mindfulnessforsuccess

I hope to see you there!

Recommended Reading for You:

If you are interested in Self-Development, Emotional Intelligence, Psychology, Social Dynamics, NLP, Soft Skills and related topics, you might be interested in previewing or downloading my other books:

Communication Skills Training: A Practical Guide to Improving Your Social Intelligence, Presentation, Persuasion and Public Speaking

Do You Know How To Communicate With People Effectively, Avoid Conflicts and Get What You Want From Life?

...It's mostly about what you say, but also about WHEN, WHY and HOW you say it.

Do The Things You Usually Say Help You, Or Maybe Hold You Back?

Have you ever considered **how many times you intuitively felt that maybe you lost something important or crucial, simply**

because you unwittingly said or did something, which put somebody off? Maybe it was a misfortunate word, bad formulation, inappropriate joke, forgotten name, huge misinterpretation, awkward conversation or a strange tone of your voice?

Maybe you assumed that you knew exactly what a particular concept meant for another person and you stopped asking questions?

Maybe you could not listen carefully or could not stay silent for a moment? **How many times have you wanted to achieve something, negotiate better terms, or ask for a promotion and failed miserably?**

It's time to put that to an end with the help of this book.

Lack of communication skills is exactly what ruins most peoples' lives.

If you don't know how to communicate properly, you are going to have problems both in your intimate and family relationships.

You are going to be ineffective in work and business situations. It's going to be troublesome managing employees or getting what you want from your boss or your clients on a daily basis. Overall, **effective communication is like an engine oil which makes your life run smoothly, getting you wherever you want to be.** There are very few areas in life in which you can succeed in the long run without this crucial skill.

What Will You Learn With This Book?

-What Are The **Most Common Communication Obstacles** Between People And How To Avoid Them

-How To Express Anger And Avoid Conflicts

-What Are **The Most 8 Important Questions You Should Ask Yourself** If You Want To Be An Effective Communicator?

-**5 Most Basic and Crucial** Conversational Fixes

-How To Deal With Difficult and Toxic People

-Phrases to **Purge from Your Dictionary** (And What to Substitute Them With)

-The Subtle Art of **Giving and Receiving Feedback**

-Rapport, the **Art of Excellent Communication**

-How to Use Metaphors to **Communicate Better** And **Connect With People**

-What Metaprograms and Meta Models Are and How Exactly To Make Use of Them To **Become A Polished Communicator**

-How To Read Faces and **How to Effectively Predict Future Behaviors**

-How to Finally Start **Remembering Names**

-How to Have a Great Public Presentation

-How To Create Your Own **Unique Personality** in Business (and Everyday Life)

-Effective Networking

Direct Buy Link:
http://tinyurl.com/iancommunicationkindle

Paperback version:

http://tinyurl.com/iancommunicationpaperback

Emotional Intelligence: A Practical Guide to Making Friends with Your Emotions and Raising Your EQ

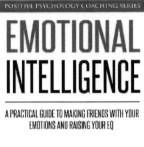

IAN TUHOVSKY

Do you believe your life would be healthier, happier and even better, if you had more practical strategies to regulate your own emotions?

Most people agree with that.

Or, more importantly:

do you believe you'd be healthier and happier if everyone who you live with had the strategies to regulate their emotions?

...right?

The truth is not too many people actually realize what EQ is really all about and what causes its popularity to grow constantly.

Scientific research conducted by many American and European Universities prove that the **'common' intelligence responses account for only less than 20% of our life achievements and successes, while the other more than 80% depends on the emotional intelligence.** To put it roughly: **either you are emotionally intelligent, or you're doomed to mediocrity, at best.**

As opposed to the popular image, emotionally intelligent people are not the ones who react impulsively and spontaneously, or who act lively and fiery in all types of social environments.

Emotionally intelligent people are open to new experiences, can show feelings adequate to the situation, either good or bad, and find it easy to socialize with other people and establish new contacts. They handle stress well, say 'no' easily, realistically assess the achievements of themselves or others, and are not afraid of constructive criticism and taking calculated risks. **They are the people of success.** Unfortunately, this perfect model of an emotionally intelligent person is extremely rare in our modern times.

Sadly nowadays, **the amount of emotional problems in the world is increasing at an alarming rate.** We are getting richer, but less and less happy. Depression, suicide, relationship breakdowns, loneliness of choice, fear of closeness, addictions - this is the clear evidence we are getting increasingly worse when it comes to dealing with our emotions.

Emotional Intelligence is a SKILL, and can be learned through constant practice and training, just like riding a bike or swimming!

This book is stuffed with lots of effective exercises, helpful info and practical ideas.

Every chapter covers different areas of emotional intelligence and shows you, **step by step**, what exactly you can do to **develop your EQ** and become the **better version of yourself**.

I will show you how freeing yourself from the domination of the left-sided brain thinking can contribute to your inner transformation – **the emotional revolution that will help you redefine who you are and what you really want from life!**

In This Book I'll Show You:
-What Is Emotional Intelligence and What Does EQ Consist Of?
-How to **Observe and Express** your Emotions
-How to **Release Negative Emotions** and **Empower the Positive Ones**
-How To Deal With Your **Internal Dialogues**
-How To **Deal With The Past**
-**How to Forgive** Yourself and How to Forgive Others
-How to Free Yourself from **Other People's Opinions and Judgments**
-What Are "Submodalities" and How Exactly You Can Use Them to **Empower Yourself** and **Get Rid of Stress**
-The Nine Things You Need to **Stop Doing to Yourself**
-How to Examine Your Thoughts

-**Internal Conflicts** Troubleshooting Technique

-The Lost Art of Asking Yourself the Right Questions

and **Discovering Your True Self!**

-How to Create Rich Visualizations

-LOTS of practical exercises from the mighty arsenal of psychology, family therapy, NLP etc.

-**And Many, Many More!**

Direct Buy Link: http://tinyurl.com/ianeqkindle

Paperback version: http://tinyurl.com/ianeqpaperback

Buddhism: Beginner's Guide: Bring Peace and Happiness To Your Everyday Life

Buddhism is one of the most practical and simple belief systems on this planet and it has greatly helped me on my way to become a better person in every aspect possible. In this book I will show you what happened and how it was.

No matter if you are totally green when it comes to Buddha's teachings or maybe you have already heard

something about them - this book will help you systematize your knowledge and will inspire you to learn more and to take steps to make your life positively better!

I invite you to take this beautiful journey into the graceful and meaningful world of Buddhism with me today!

Direct link: http://tinyurl.com/ianbuddhismkindle

Paperback version:
http://tinyurl.com/ianbuddhismpaperback

Meditation for Beginners: How to Meditate (As An Ordinary Person!) to Relieve Stress and be Successful

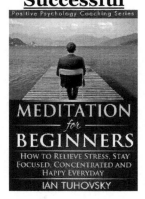

Meditation doesn't have to be about crystals, hypnotic folk music and incense sticks!

Forget about sitting in unnatural and uncomfortable positions while going "ommmmm...."

It is not necessarily a club full of yoga masters, Shaolin monks, hippies and new-agers.

It is super practical and universal practice which can improve your overall brain performance and happiness.

When meditating, you take a step back from actively thinking your thoughts, and instead, see them for what they are. The reason why meditation is helpful in reducing stress and attaining peace is that it gives your over-active conscious a break.

Just like your body needs it, your mind does too!

I give you the gift of peace that I was able to attain through present moment awareness.

Direct link: http://tinyurl.com/ianmeditationkindle

Paperback version:
http://tinyurl.com/ianmeditationpaperback

Gain Self-Confidence Fast With NLP

In this short read you'll learn about the **most effective NLP tools in the context of permanent self-esteem boost,** but also my mindset, the right approach that actually works and I'll share few personal stories that will motivate you. I'll tell you how to stick to your personal change plan and how to start a journey towards being a better person!

Zen: Beginner's Guide: Happy, Peaceful and Focused Lifestyle for Everyone

Contrary to popular belief, Zen is not a discipline reserved for monks practicing Kung Fu. Although there is some truth to this idea, Zen is a practice that is applicable, useful, and pragmatic for anyone to study regardless of what religion you follow (or don't follow).

Zen is the practice of studying your subconscious and **seeing your true nature.**

The purpose of this work is to show you how to apply and utilize the teachings and essence of Zen in everyday life in the Western society. I'm not really an "absolute truth seeker" unworldly type of person - I just believe in practical plans and blueprints that actually help in living a better life. Of course I will tell you about the origin of Zen and the traditional ways of practicing it, but I will also show you my side of things, my personal point of view and translation of many Zen truths through a more "contemporary" and practical language.

It is a "modern Zen lifestyle" type of book.

What You Will Read About:

- Where Did Zen Come From? - A short history and explanation of Zen
- What Does Zen Teach? - The major teachings and precepts of Zen
- Various Zen meditation techniques that are applicable and practical for everyone!
- The benefits of a Zen lifestyle
- What Zen Buddhism is NOT?
- How to slow down and start enjoying your life
- How to accept everything and lose nothing
- Why being alone can be beneficial
- Why pleasure is NOT happiness
- Six Ways to Practically Let Go
- How to de-clutter your life and live simply
- "Mindfulness on Steroids"
- How to Take Care of your Awareness and Focus
- Where to start and how to practice Zen as a regular person
- And many other interesting concepts...

I invite you to take this journey into the peaceful world of Zen Buddhism with me today!

Direct Buy Link: <u>http://tinyurl.com/ianzenkindle</u>

<u>Paperback version: http://tinyurl.com/ianzenpaperback</u>

About The Author

Author's blog: **www.mindfulnessforsuccess.com**
Amazon Author Page: http://www.amazon.com/Ian-Tuhovsky/e/B00IGQ4V1Y

Hi! I'm Ian...

. . . and I am interested in life. In the study of having an awesome and passionate life, which I believe is within the reach of practically everyone. I'm not a mentor or a guru. I'm just a guy who always knew there was more than we are told. I managed to turn my life around from way below my expectations to a really satisfying life, and now I want to share this fascinating journey with you so that you can do it, too.

I was born and raised somewhere in Eastern Europe, where Polar Bears eat people on the streets, we munch on snow instead of ice-cream and there's only vodka instead of tap water, but since I make a living out of several different businesses, I move to a new country every couple of months. I also work as an HR consultant for various European companies.

I love self-development, traveling, recording music and providing value by helping others. I passionately read and write about social psychology, sociology, NLP, meditation, mindfulness, eastern philosophy, emotional intelligence, time management, communication skills and all of the topics related to conscious self-development and being the most awesome version of yourself.

Breathe. Relax. Feel that you're alive and smile. And never hesitate to contact me!

Printed in Great Britain
by Amazon.co.uk, Ltd.,
Marston Gate.